Heinemann First
ENCYCLOPEDIA

Volume 5
Fra-Ind

Heinemann Library
Chicago, Illinois

Series Editors: Rebecca and Stephen Vickers, Gianna Williams
Author Team: Rob Alcraft, Catherine Chambers, Sabrina Crewe, Jim Drake, Fred Martin, Angela Royston, Jane Shuter, Roger Thomas, Rebecca Vickers, Stephen Vickers

This revised and expanded edition produced for Heinemann Library by Discovery Books.
Photo research by Katherine Smith and Rachel Tisdale
Designed by Keith Williams, Michelle Lisseter, and Gecko
Illustrations by Stefan Chabluk and Mark Bergin

Originated by Ambassador Litho Limited
Printed in China by WKT Company Limited

10 09 08 07 06
10 9 8 7 6 5 4 3 2

Library of Congress Cataloging-in-Publication Data

Heinemann first encyclopedia.
    p.   cm.
    Summary: A fourteen-volume encyclopedia covering animals, plants, countries, transportation, science, ancient civilizations, US states, US presidents, and world history
     ISBN 1-4034-7112-6 (v. 5 : lib. bdg.)
     1. Children's encyclopedias and dictionaries.
I. Heinemann Library (Firm)
AG5.H45 2005
031—dc22   2005006176

Acknowledgments
Cover: Cover photographs of a desert, an electric guitar, a speedboat, an iceberg, a man on a camel, cactus flowers, and the Colosseum at night reproduced with permission of Corbis. Cover photograph of the Taj Mahal reproduced with permission of Digital Stock. Cover photograph of an x-ray of a man, and the penguins reproduced with permission of Digital Vision. Cover photographs of a giraffe, the Leaning Tower of Pisa, the Statue of Liberty, a white owl, a cactus, a butterfly, a saxophone, an astronaut, cars at night, and a circuit board reproduced with permission of Getty Images/Photodisc. Cover photograph of Raglan Castle reproduced with permission of Peter Evans; J. Allan Cash Ltd, pp. 6, 9, 10, 16, 17, 18, 30, 33, 39, 41, 44, 46, 48; Ancient Art and Architecture/Mary Jelcliffe, p. 29; Trevor Clifford Photography, p. 25 bottom; Bruce Coleman/Wayne Larkinen, p. 28 top; Richard Day, p. 38 bottom; Hulton Archive/Getty Images, p. 4 top; Hulton Deutsch, pp. 27 top, 36 top; The Hutchison Library/Sarah Errington, p. 20; The Hutchison Library, p. 34; S. Alden/PhotoLink, p. 22; Oxford Scientific Films/Jen and Den Bartlett, p. 13; G.I. Bernard, p. 5 bottom; Mike Birkhead, p. 28 bottom; Roger Brown, p. 7 bottom; Bruce Davidson, p. 31 top; Tim Davis, p. 11 top; Jack Dermid, p. 5 top; Jerry Driendl/Taxi, p. 8; William H. Edwards/The Image Bank, p. 47; Jim Frazer, p. 23 bottom; David Fritts, p. 12 bottom; Philip Gould/Corbis, p. 45 bottom; Tim Jackson, p. 11 bottom; Paul Kay, p. 19 bottom; Steve Liss/Time Life Pictures/Getty Images, p. 45 top; Sean Morris, p. 15 bottom; Owen Newman, p. 26; Richard Parkwood, p. 31 bottom; PhotoDisk, p. 14 bottom; Ralph Rheinhold, p. 35 top; James Robinson, p. 12 top; Brian Snyder/Reuters/Corbis, p. 14 top; Survival Anglia/T. Andrewartha, p. 21 bottom; Survival Anglia/Claude Steelman, p. 21 top; Tony Stone Worldwide/Cameron Davidson, p. 40 top; Philip Tull, p. 35 bottom; Peter Ward, p. 7 top; Martin Wendler, p. 15 top; M. Wilding, p. 23 top; Scenics of America/PhotoLink, p. 42; PhotoDisk, p. 43; Science Photo Library/Agema Infrared Systems, p. 25 top; Science Photo Library/NASA, p. 40 bottom; Stock Montage/Stock Montage/Getty Images, p. 4 bottom; T.C. Nature, p. 38 top; Ariel Skelley/Corbis, p. 32 bottom; Deep Light Industries, p. 24; Alan Hicks, p. 27 bottom; Michael S. Yamashita/Corbis, p. 32 top; Zefa, p. 36 bottom.

Welcome to
Heinemann First Encyclopedia

What is an encyclopedia?

An encyclopedia is an information book. It gives the most important facts about many different subjects. This encyclopedia has been written for children who are using an encyclopedia for the first time. It covers many of the subjects from school and others you may find interesting.

What is in this encyclopedia?

In this encyclopedia, each topic is called an *entry*. There is one page of information for every entry. The entries in this encyclopedia explain

- animals
- plants
- dinosaurs
- countries
- geography
- history
- world religions
- music
- art
- transportation
- science
- technology
- states
- famous Americans

How to use this encyclopedia

This encyclopedia has thirteen books called *volumes*. The first twelve volumes contain entries. The entries are all in alphabetical order. This means that Volume 1 starts with entries that begin with the letter A and Volume 12 ends with entries that begin with the letter Z. Volume 13 is the index volume. It also has other interesting information.

Here are two entries that show you what you can find on a page:

This is the letter that the entry starts with.

Fact boxes give you details about the topic.

The "see also" line tells you where to find other related information.

Did You Know? boxes have fun or interesting bits of information.

The Fact File tells you important facts and figures.

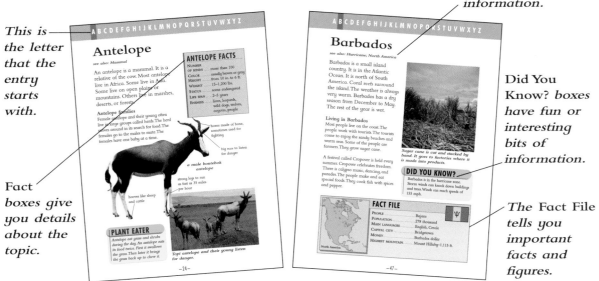

Franklin, Benjamin

see also: Constitution, Lightning

Benjamin Franklin was an inventor, writer, and a founder of the United States of America.

Young Franklin
He was born in Boston, in the colony of Massachusetts, on January 17, 1706. He was the tenth of seventeen children. When Franklin was twelve, he started working for his brother, a printer.

Franklin went to Philadelphia and opened his own printing shop. In 1732 he started to publish *Poor Richard's Almanack*. The almanac had advice, news, and useful information. It made Franklin famous.

Benjamin Franklin

Representing his country
Franklin went to England before the American Revolution. He represented Americans and defended their rights. Franklin came back to America and was a leader during the Revolution. Franklin helped write the Declaration of Independence. When the Revolution was over, he went to France to represent the new United States of America. Franklin helped create the U.S. Constitution in 1787. He died in 1790.

Thomas Jefferson wrote the Declaration of Independence with help from Benjamin Franklin.

DID YOU KNOW?
Benjamin Franklin did many useful things. He opened a library, a fire department, a hospital, and a school. He invented the lightning rod, a stove, and glasses called bifocals. Franklin organized the post office for all the colonies.

Frog

see also: Amphibian, Metamorphosis, Toad

A frog is an amphibian. It is born in the water but spends most of its life on land. Different kinds of frogs live all over the world. A few frogs can climb trees. Most frogs hide during the day. They come out at night.

Frog families

A frog lays about 2,000–4,000 eggs in spring. The eggs are laid in a pond. The eggs are called frogspawn. These eggs hatch as tadpoles. Most frogs do not take care of their tadpoles. Over a few weeks or months the tadpoles change into frogs. Frogs in cold countries hibernate in mud or in leaves during the winter.

FROG FACTS

NUMBER OF KINDS	about 2,600
COLOR	Poisonous frogs are brightly colored. Most other frogs are brown or green.
LENGTH	up to 12 inches
STATUS	common
LIFE SPAN	5 to 12 years
ENEMIES	Foxes, herons, fish, and ducks eat frogs. Ducks, newts, and dragonfly larvae eat tadpoles.

eyes that look two ways for danger

long, sticky tongue to catch insects

springy back legs to jump

webbed feet for swimming

an American river frog

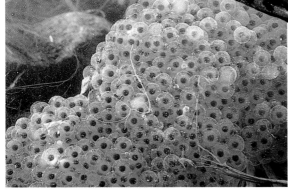

The dark spot in each egg can turn into a tadpole.

PLANT, INSECT, AND MEAT EATER

Tadpoles eat water weeds. Bigger tadpoles eat insects. Adult frogs eat flies and slugs.

Fuel

see also: Electricity, Energy, Fossil

A fuel is anything that gives off heat or other energy. Natural gas, oil, and coal are all fuels.

Types of fuel

Natural gas is underground. A deep hole, called a well, is drilled into the ground. The gas rushes up out of the hole. Gas is used for cooking and heating. It is also used for making electricity in a power plant.

Oil is often found in the same places as gas. Crude oil is pumped from underground. Gasoline, diesel fuel, and heating oil all come from crude oil.

Coal comes from the ground. Most of it is burned in power plants to make electricity.

DID YOU KNOW?

In some places people use a machine that makes fuel out of cow manure.

Peat is partly decayed plant matter. It is dug from the ground and dried. Peat can be burned as fuel.

People and fuels

One day all the fuels in the ground will be used up. Scientists are trying to find ways to use fuels that will not run out. These are renewable fuels. Two sources of renewable energy are the sun and the wind. They will not run out like fossil fuels from the ground.

This is an oil refinery in Kuwait. An oil refinery turns black, sticky crude oil into useful fuels.

Fungus

see also: Plant

A fungus is a living thing. It is like a plant, but it does not have leaves, stems, or real roots. Fungi include mushrooms, toadstools, yeasts, and molds. Fungi grow almost everywhere. They grow on land and in water.

FUNGI FACTS

NUMBER OF KINDS	about 100 thousand
LARGEST FUNGI ...	up to 12 inches across
LIFE SPAN	up to many years
ENEMIES	bacteria, special chemicals called fungicides

a rain forest fungus

Life of a fungus

The main part of the fungus is under the ground. Tiny threads take in food from the soil. A mushroom is the fruit of a fungus. A fungus produces spores instead of seeds. The spores are scattered by the wind or by animals. Some fungi grow on living plants and animals.

gills underneath the mushroom contain spores

Some fungi cause diseases in people, animals, and plants. Other fungi are useful. Fungi make bread rise. They make yogurt and some cheeses. Fungi also make the medicine called penicillin. Some mushrooms can be eaten. Other mushrooms and toadstools are poisonous.

Tiny fungi grow in forest leaf litter. Scientists who study fungi are called mycologists.

Georgia

see also: United States of America

Georgia is a state in the southeastern United States of America. The Blue Ridge Mountains are in the north. Central Georgia has hills. The land is lower in the south and along the coast. Georgia is warm and humid. It rains a lot in the state.

This is a view of Savannah's waterfront.

Life in Georgia

Georgia is the largest state east of the Mississippi River. Savannah is a beautiful old city in Georgia. It was an important port in colonial America. It is still an important port today. Products are shipped all over the world from Savannah.

Peanuts are an important crop in Georgia. *Nguba* is an African word for "peanut." Some people call Georgia the "goober" state because of all the

DID YOU KNOW?

The Sea Islands are along Georgia's coastline. Sea turtles live around the Sea Islands. At night, they lay their eggs on the islands' beaches.

peanuts grown there. Farmers also grow cotton and corn. Many people work in factories in Georgia. The state's factories produce more paper than those in any other state. Other factories make textiles and clothes.

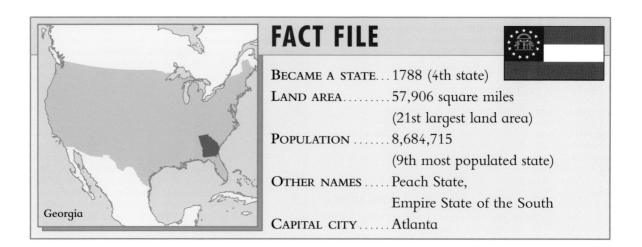

Georgia

FACT FILE

BECAME A STATE...	1788 (4th state)
LAND AREA.........	57,906 square miles (21st largest land area)
POPULATION	8,684,715 (9th most populated state)
OTHER NAMES	Peach State, Empire State of the South
CAPITAL CITY	Atlanta

Germany

see also: Europe

Germany is a country in the middle of Europe. The north of Germany is lowland. The center and south have hills and mountains. Big rivers flow through Germany from south to north. The weather is mostly warm in summer. It can be very cold with snow in winter.

Living in Germany

Most Germans live and work in its big cities.

There are special traditions and festivals in most towns and villages. Some festivals are 600 years old. One of the most famous festivals reminds people of the "Pied Piper of Hamelin." The pied piper is believed to have led the rats out of the town of Hamelin.

DID YOU KNOW?

From 1948 to 1990 Germany was divided into two countries. The western half was called the German Federal Republic and the eastern half was the German Democratic Republic.

Many towns and cities in Germany have open squares. This open square is in the Romer area of Frankfurt.

Europe

FACT FILE

PEOPLE	Germans
POPULATION	about 82 million
MAIN LANGUAGE	German
CAPITAL CITY	Berlin
MONEY	Euro
HIGHEST MOUNTAIN	Zugspitze–9,725 feet
LONGEST RIVER	Rhine River–820 miles

Ghana

see also: Africa

Ghana is a country in west Africa. It is mostly hot lowland. It is cooler in the hills in the east and west. The world's largest artificial lake is in Ghana. It is called Lake Volta.

Living in Ghana

Most people in Ghana live near the coast. More than half of the people work on farms.

Rice, yams, and cassava are grown. They are eaten with meat, fish, and peanut stews. Many Ghanaians wear clothes made of *kente*. This is a special, many-colored cloth. The cloth is sold in the markets. It is also sold to other countries.

Ghana also has small factories and mines. The cocoa beans they grow are sent all over the world to be made into chocolate.

Traders sell their produce in local markets. This market is in Kasoa, in the center of Ghana.

DID YOU KNOW?

Ghana was once part of an area called the Gold Coast. It took the name *Ghana* when it became an independent country in 1957.

Africa

FACT FILE

PEOPLE	Ghanaians
POPULATION	about 20 million
MAIN LANGUAGES	English, African languages
CAPITAL CITY	Accra
MONEY	Cedi
HIGHEST MOUNTAIN	Mount Afadjado—2,905 feet
LONGEST RIVER	Volta River—950 miles

Giraffe

see also: Mammal

A giraffe is the tallest land mammal in the world. It lives on the grassy plains of Africa. Every giraffe has a different color pattern.

male giraffe's horns used for fighting

A giraffe spreads its legs and bends low to get a drink.

Giraffe families

A male giraffe is called a bull. A female giraffe is called a cow. A cow has one baby at a time. The baby is called a calf. The females look after each other's young. Giraffes do not stay in one special group. They move from group to group. They do not build a home. Bull giraffes fight. The winner of the fight becomes the head bull.

GIRAFFE FACTS

NUMBER OF KINDS	1
COLOR	brown, yellow, and white
LENGTH	about 6 feet
HEIGHT	up to 17 feet
WEIGHT	up to 4,200 lbs.
STATUS	endangered
LIFE SPAN	about 25 years
ENEMIES	hyenas, leopards, and wild dogs

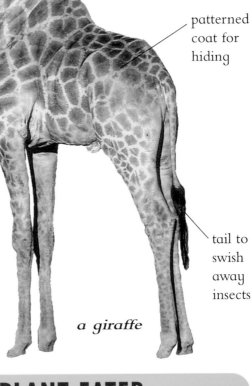

long neck to reach high into trees

long tongue to pull leaves from trees

patterned coat for hiding

tail to swish away insects

a giraffe

PLANT EATER

A giraffe eats leaves and shoots from tall trees. It also eats grass.

Goat

see also: Mammal

A goat is a medium-sized mammal. People keep goats for their milk, meat, and wool. Wild goats live in some mountain areas.

Goat families

A male goat is called a billy goat or a buck. A female goat is called a nanny goat or a doe. A nanny goat usually has two babies at a time. A young goat is called a kid. Farm goats are kept together in groups called herds.

GOAT FACTS

NUMBER OF KINDS	600 (mainly farm goats)
COLOR	brown, black, white
HEIGHT	18 inches to 4 feet
WEIGHT	20 to 300 lbs.
STATUS	common
LIFE SPAN	8 to 10 years
ENEMIES	wolves, bears, lions, leopards

horns for fighting

billy and nanny goats may have beards

shaggy hair that can be woven into wool

an American mountain goat

strong legs to climb steep cliffs

Mountain goats are very sure-footed. Even the very young goats can safely trot along narrow ledges.

PLANT EATER

A goat eats all kinds of plants and fruit. It even eats spiky thorn bushes. Farm goats will eat almost anything. They will even eat the labels off cans.

Goose

see also: Bird

A goose is a large bird. It lives near water in all but the coldest parts of the world. Some geese are raised by farmers. Geese are raised for their meat, eggs, and feathers.

Goose families

A male is called a gander. A female is called a goose. A baby is called a gosling. The gander and goose build a nest on the ground. They fill the nest with grass. The goose lays from three to eleven eggs. After the eggs hatch, both parents feed the goslings.

Many kinds of geese migrate long distances. They travel each fall to spend the winter in warmer places. They travel in groups called flocks. The flock flies in a big V-shape. The geese take turns being the leader of the flock.

GOOSE FACTS

NUMBER OF KINDS	more than 30
COLOR	usually gray, white, or black
LENGTH	up to 4 feet
WEIGHT	up to 11 lbs.
STATUS	common
LIFE SPAN	up to 20 years
ENEMIES	foxes, people

sharp-edged beak for cutting grass

waterproof feathers for swimming

strong wings for flying and fighting

webbed feet for swimming

a Canada goose

PLANT EATER

A goose eats plants found in the water and on land.

Snow goose goslings keep warm in a nest lined with their mother's down feathers.

Government

see also: Constitution, Executive Branch, Judicial Branch, Legislative Branch

Government is the system used to run a nation, region, or city. A government is made up of people who manage things for everyone else in their nation, region or city.

Types of government

Different nations have different types of government. Some nations are monarchies. They have rulers who are monarchs, such as kings or queens. Monarchs are not elected. Monarchs have their power passed down to them from their parents.

Other nations have a communist system of government. In communist nations, everything is owned by the government. Everyone is supposed to live the same way and share everything.

Political parties in a democracy hold rallies to boost support from voters.

Government in the United States

The United States is a democracy. That means Americans choose who governs them by voting in elections. The person with the most votes wins.

What does a government do?

A government's job is to make laws and other decisions. Governments also collect money in taxes. They use the money to keep schools, police departments, and fire stations running. They fix roads and build public facilities. National governments defend their nations with military forces.

The U.S. government is based on Capitol Hill, in Washington, D.C.

DID YOU KNOW?

In the United States, each state has its own government that works together with the national government. This system is called federalism.

Grasshopper

see also: Insect

A grasshopper is an insect.
It uses its long back legs to
jump. It rubs its legs or wings
to make a clicking or whirring
noise. Grasshoppers live in most
parts of the world. They do not
live in the Arctic or Antarctica.

Grasshopper families

A grasshopper lays its eggs in the soil.
A young grasshopper hatches from the
egg. The young grasshopper is called
a larva. The larva grows and sheds
its skin many times. It slowly
changes into an adult with wings.
Big groups of grasshoppers are
called swarms.

GRASSHOPPER FACTS

NUMBER OF KINDS	about 10 thousand
COLOR	usually green
LENGTH	up to 4 inches
STATUS	common
LIFE SPAN	up to about 9 months
ENEMIES	birds, snakes, frogs, spiders, beetles, people

PLANT EATER

Some grasshoppers eat only one kind of plant. Others eat any plant they find.

a short-horned grasshopper

long antennae to smell and feel

strong mouth to chew through leaves

ears on the knees of a long-horned grasshopper

long back legs to jump almost 40 times its own length

These young grasshoppers have a bright warning color. The color may keep away predators.

Greece

see also: Europe; Greece, Ancient

Greece is a country in southeast Europe. Greece has many islands in the Mediterranean Sea.

Living in Greece

Half of the people of Greece live in small towns and villages. Many houses are painted white. The white color reflects the hot sun. This helps keep the inside cool. Olives, grapes, potatoes, and sugar beets are grown on small farms.

People from all over the world visit Greece. They enjoy the hot, sunny summers. They visit the ruins of ancient Greece. Many Greeks work in hotels and museums. Some Greeks have boats to carry people and goods between the many islands.

Many small fishing boats work around the Greek coast and islands.

DID YOU KNOW?

Greece has a big shipping fleet. Ships from Greece sail all over the world. They carry goods such as grain and oil.

Europe

FACT FILE

PEOPLE	Greeks
POPULATION	about 10 million
MAIN LANGUAGE	Greek
CAPITAL CITY	Athens
MONEY	Euro
HIGHEST MOUNTAIN	Mount Olympus—9,574 feet
LONGEST RIVER	Aliakmon River—180 miles

Greece, Ancient

see also: Greece, Olympic Games

The civilization of ancient Greece began about 800 B.C. It lasted until about 146 B.C. when the Romans began to take over.

What were the ancient Greeks like?

The ancient Greeks lived in city-states. A city-state was a city and the land around the city. Each city-state had its own government. Some city-states had one leader. In other city-states the men voted. They decided how to run the government. All men had to fight when a city-state went to war. Women stayed home with the children.

The ancient Greeks believed in and prayed to many gods and goddesses. The people gave the gods and goddesses presents to keep them happy.

For what are the ancient Greeks known?

The ancient Greeks are well-known for their buildings, statues, and painted vases. Ancient Greek thinkers, writers, and inventors are still studied and remembered.

KEY DATES

800 B.C.	city-states begin
776 B.C.	first Olympic Games held
700 B.C.	Greek alphabet invented
400 B.C.	Greeks begin to use mathematics
336–323 B.C.	Alexander the Great rules all of Greece
146 B.C.	Greece becomes part of the Roman Empire

The ancient ruins of the Acropolis are in the city of Athens. The Acropolis was a group of buildings on a hill. The largest building was the temple called the Parthenon.

Guatemala

see also: Maya, North America

Guatemala is a country in Central America. There are lowlands near the coast and in the north. Mountains cross the middle of Guatemala. The mountains have very rich soil. There are also active volcanoes in the mountains. Rain forest covers the northern part of the country.

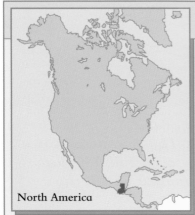

Mayan people weave brightly colored cloth and rugs.

Living in Guatemala

Most people in Guatemala live in small towns and villages. They live where the soil is good for farming. The farmers grow coffee, sugar, bananas, corn, and beans. The chicozapunte tree grows in the northern rain forest. The sap of this tree is used to make chewing gum.

The people in Guatemala eat mixed beans and rice. They eat salads made of avocados, tomatoes, and onions. The bread they eat is made from corn.

DID YOU KNOW?

More than 1,000 years ago, northern Guatemala was part of the ancient Mayan civilization. Even today most of the people are Mayan Indians.

FACT FILE

North America

PEOPLE	Guatemalans
POPULATION	about 14 million
MAIN LANGUAGE	Spanish
CAPITAL CITY	Guatemala City
MONEY	Quetzal
HIGHEST MOUNTAIN	Volcán Tajumulco—13,840 feet
LONGEST RIVER	Rio Salinas—298 miles

Gull

see also: Bird, Seabird

A gull is a seabird. A gull can fly. It can float on water. A gull cannot dive underwater. Many gulls move away from the sea. They live on lakes or rivers. Gulls are found all over the world.

GULL FACTS

NUMBER OF KINDS	43
COLOR	white, gray, and black
LENGTH	up to 26 inches
STATUS	common
LIFE SPAN	about 30 years
ENEMIES	rats, people

Gull families

Gulls choose a partner. The partners usually stay together for life. Some gulls build round nests on the beach. Other gulls lay eggs on cliff ledges. A female gull lays two or three eggs once a year. A baby gull is called a chick. Both parents feed the chick. A chick pecks at the adults' beaks to let them know it needs food.

curved beak to pull off bits of food

a herring gull

waterproof feathers to keep dry

webbed feet for walking on sand and paddling through water

Herring gull chicks have splotchy markings. The markings help them hide from enemies.

PLANT, INSECT, AND MEAT EATER

A gull eats almost anything it finds. It even eats the meat of dead seals and whales. A gull breaks open the hard shells of mussels and crabs by dropping the shells to the ground from the sky.

Pendleton Community Library

Haiti

see also: North America

Haiti is a country. It is on part of the island of Hispaniola. It is in the Caribbean Sea. Haiti has mountains with small valleys. It has hot coastal plains. The climate is hot and wet all year round.

Living in Haiti

Most people in Haiti live in the country. They live on very small farms. They grow coffee, sisal, sugar cane, and cocoa. These crops are sold to other countries. Farmers also grow corn, cassava, sweet potatoes, and beans. Cloth is made in factories.

The life style of the people is called Creole. Creole is a mix of African and French life styles. The food, houses, and music are Creole. The people follow both old African religions and Christianity.

Haiti has a carnival time. The people dress in costumes. They dance through the streets in big parades.

DID YOU KNOW?

King Christophe of Haiti began using gourds as money about 200 years ago. A gourd is a hard-skinned fruit. It is like a pumpkin. Haiti uses coins now, but they still call the money *gourde*.

North America

FACT FILE

PEOPLE	Haitians
POPULATION	7 million
MAIN LANGUAGES	French, Haitian Creole
CAPITAL CITY	Port-au-Prince
MONEY	Gourde
HIGHEST MOUNTAIN	Chaîne de la Selle—8,796 feet
LONGEST RIVER	Artibonite River—100 miles

Hare

see also: Mammal, Rabbit

A hare is a mammal. It looks like a rabbit. It has long ears and long legs. Hares are also called jackrabbits. Hares live on grassland. Hares that live in snowy places have white fur in the winter.

Hare families

A male hare is called a jack. A female hare is called a doe. The doe has from two to four babies at a time. The babies are called leverets. The doe scrapes a small hollow in the grass. The nest is called a form. The doe puts grass in the form to make it soft. She makes a form for each leveret after they are born. The leverets leave their mother when they are three weeks old. Then they live on their own.

HARE FACTS

NUMBER OF KINDS	44 hares and rabbits
COLOR	brown, gray, or white
LENGTH	about 24 inches
WEIGHT	about 11 lbs.
STATUS	common
LIFE SPAN	about 5 years
ENEMIES	foxes, eagles

sensitive nose to smell danger

long ears to help the hare keep cool and to listen for danger

a black-tailed jackrabbit

long legs to jump and to run up to 40 mph

strong front paws for fighting

These European hare leverets are warming themselves in the sun.

PLANT EATER

A hare feeds at night on grass, roots, bark, and grain.

Hawaii

see also: United States of America

Hawaii is a state in the United States of America. It is in the Pacific Ocean. Hawaii is a group of islands that were once volcanoes. Some volcanoes still erupt. The weather in Hawaii is warm. There is a lot of rain.

Life in Hawaii

Hawaii is a long way from all other communities in the world. It even has its own time zone. The state is 2,400 miles from the United States' mainland. The first people to settle in Hawaii long ago were Polynesians from other islands in the Pacific Ocean. Today, Hawaiians come from many cultures.

Most people in Hawaii live in towns and cities. Many of them work in tourism. Tourists like to visit Hawaii's many beaches.

Ancient sculptures sit on the beach at Pu'uhonua o Honaunau National Historical Park, Hawaii.

DID YOU KNOW?

The world's two biggest telescopes are in Hawaii. They can look far into space. The world's largest windmill is there, too. The windmill uses wind to make energy. It can make enough electricity for a thousand homes.

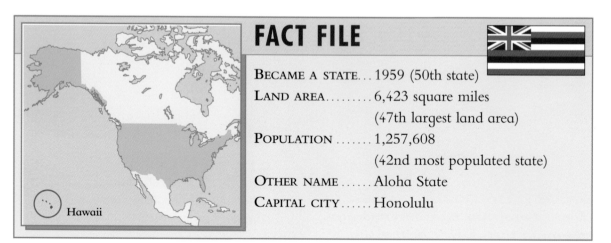

FACT FILE

BECAME A STATE... 1959 (50th state)

LAND AREA......... 6,423 square miles
(47th largest land area)

POPULATION 1,257,608
(42nd most populated state)

OTHER NAME ...... Aloha State

CAPITAL CITY ...... Honolulu

Hawaii

Hawk

see also: Bird

A hawk is a bird of prey. It catches and kills animals to eat. There are many kinds of hawks. They live all over the world except in Antarctica.

Hawk families

A female hawk lays eggs in a nest. The chicks hatch and stay in the nest. They are fed by the parent birds until they can fly. Hawk nests can be on a cliff, in a tree, or on the ground.

HAWK FACTS

NUMBER OF KINDS....	about 200
COLOR......	usually brown or gray
LENGTH.....	10 to 28 inches
WEIGHT.....	3 oz. to 4 lbs.
STATUS......	common
LIFE SPAN...	up to 25 years
ENEMIES.....	larger birds, people

broad wings to soar through the air

good eyesight to spot small animals from high in the air

sharp, hooked beak to tear up food

curved talons to grasp and carry prey

tail to steer while soaring

a buzzard

The crested hawk feeds her chicks insects and frogs.

INSECT AND MEAT EATER

Hawks eat mice, frogs, insects, and other small animals. Some hawks swallow the whole animal. Then they bring it up and spit out the fur, feathers, and bones.

Heart

see also: Blood, Human Body

The heart is a special, strong muscle. It is a pump. It pumps blood around the body. Every animal has a heart. It is in the chest of most animals.

How the heart works

The heart has four spaces. The top two spaces are called atria. They fill up with blood that has gone around the body through the veins. The atria squeeze the blood into the two spaces at the bottom of the heart. These spaces are called the ventricles. Valves in the heart let the blood go only in one direction. The valves are like doors that only open one way.

A human heart beats more than two billion times in a lifetime. The heart pumps slowly when a person is asleep. The heart pumps quickly when a person exercises.

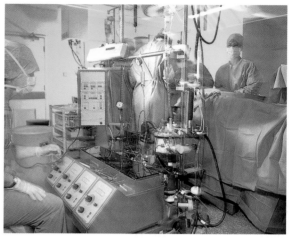

Doctors can perform operations on unhealthy hearts. Special machines do the work of the heart and lungs while the doctor operates.

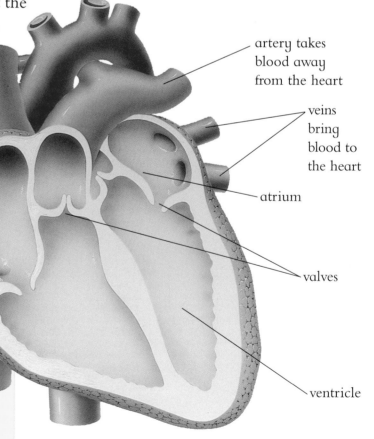

artery takes blood away from the heart

veins bring blood to the heart

atrium

valves

ventricle

the human heart

STAY HEALTHY

Eating the right food, not smoking, and getting plenty of exercise can keep the heart healthy.

Heat

see also: Energy, Fuel

Heat is a kind of energy. Heat is usually released by burning fuel. There are many types of fuel. Firewood and the food we eat are fuels.

Types of heat

Heat is important to human beings. A person can die if the body is not warm enough.

Materials called insulators keep in heat. Curtains that cover windows help to keep heat inside a house. Warm clothing in winter helps to keep a person's body from losing heat. The fur on an animal is also a very good insulator.

Materials called conductors allow heat to escape. Metals are good conductors.

People and heat

People have used heat to cook food and for warmth since humans first made fires a long time ago. Heat can also soften or melt things in order to change their shape. Metals and some plastics are shaped this way.

A special camera shows heat escaping from a house. The yellow areas show where the most heat is escaping.

Pots and pans are made of a conductor such as metal. The heat passes from the burner to the food. The handle is made of an insulator. This protects a person's hand from the heat.

Hedgehog

see also: Hibernation, Mammal

A hedgehog is a mammal. A hedgehog's body is covered in spines. A hedgehog rolls into a ball to protect itself from danger. Hedgehogs are found in woods and fields. They are found in parts of Europe, Asia, Africa, and New Zealand.

Hedgehog families

The male lives on his own. The female builds a special nest in spring or summer. She has from four to six babies. The babies leave the nest after four weeks. Hedgehogs that live in cold places hibernate all winter.

HEDGEHOG FACTS

NUMBER OF KINDS	12
COLOR	brown
LENGTH	8 to 12 inches
WEIGHT	about 25 oz.
STATUS	common
LIFE SPAN	about 6 years
ENEMIES	foxes, people

good ears to hear worms and insects

special eyes to see at night

a European hedgehog

sharp spines to protect from danger

little feet can be tucked inside to roll into a ball

long nose to find food on the ground

Hedgehog babies are born with soft spines that quickly harden.

PLANT AND INSECT EATER

A hedgehog hunts for worms and insects at night. It also likes to eat soft fruit.

Helicopter

see also: Airplane, Transportation

A helicopter is an aircraft without fixed wings. A helicopter has spinning blades called rotors. The rotors are on top of the helicopter. The rotors push the helicopter up into the air.

The first helicopters

Helicopters were first thought of hundreds of years ago. The first helicopter was built in 1907. It easily went out of control. Helicopters improved and could fly by 1937. The United States Army was the first to use helicopters. Most helicopters are still used by the military.

How we use helicopters

Helicopters can land almost anywhere. They can take off straight up into the air. They can go forwards, backwards, and sideways. They can hover over the same spot. These movements make them very useful. They can land where there is no room for an airplane to land. Helicopters rescue people from sinking ships or mountain cliffs. Helicopters are used as ambulances. They are used by the police to chase criminals.

HELICOPTER FIRSTS	
INVENTED	1907
FIRST MILITARY HELICOPTERS	1942
FIRST PASSENGER HELICOPTER	1945
FIRST TRANSATLANTIC HELICOPTER FLIGHT	1967

In 1907, Paul Cornu's double rotor machine crashed almost every time it tried to take off.

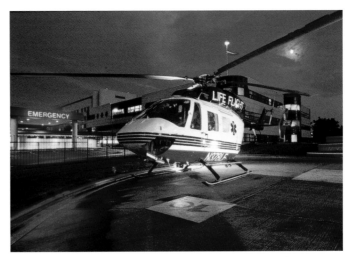

An ambulance helicopter can travel very quickly to places that other vehicles cannot reach.

Hibernation

see also: Animal, Season

Some animals have a type of winter sleep. It is called hibernation. Animals hibernate in the winter because there is not much food available when it is cold. The animal wakes up when the weather gets warmer.

What is hibernation?

Hibernation is more than just going to sleep. First, hibernating animals need to eat a lot before hibernating. The fat on their bodies will keep them alive while they sleep. They also need to hide in a safe place where enemies can't find them. While hibernating, the animal's heartbeat slows down. The animal's breathing is very shallow and slow. The animal almost looks dead. It can take days for the animal to become fully awake.

Black bears have a long winter sleep that is like hibernation.

Who hibernates?

Many different kinds of animals hibernate. Butterflies and other insects will sometimes hibernate in sheds and garages. Bats hibernate in caves and roofs where they roost. Snakes and other reptiles also hibernate. Frogs and toads bury themselves in mud or piles of leaves.

Some animals are only hiding in the winter. They are not really hibernating. Squirrels stay in their nests. They rest for most of the winter. They come out on fine, warm days.

This hedgehog has been hibernating under a pile of leaves.

Hieroglyphics

see also: Alphabet; Aztecs;
Egypt, Ancient; Maya

Hieroglyphics are a kind of
writing. Hieroglyphics use
pictures. All ancient styles of
writing used hieroglyphics.

Who used hieroglyphics?

The ancient Egyptians, the Mayas,
and the Aztecs all used hieroglyphics.
They carved them on stone. They
painted them on stone or paper.

Hieroglyphics showed real things.
It was hard to show ideas. Drawing
or carving hieroglyphics took a
long time. They were hard to learn.
The pictures had to be drawn
nearly the same way each time.
Only a few people could read
or write hieroglyphics.

What happened to hieroglyphics?

People who used hieroglyphics
began to change the pictures. They
made the pictures stand for sounds.
The sound pictures were used to
spell words. Later, alphabets replaced
hieroglyphics. Alphabets could express
words more clearly. Alphabets were
quicker and easier to learn.

KEY DATES

4000 B.C.	first alphabet is used
3000 B.C.	Egyptians begin to use hieroglyphics
A.D. 500	Maya begin to use hieroglyphics
A.D. 1200	Aztecs begin to use hieroglyphics

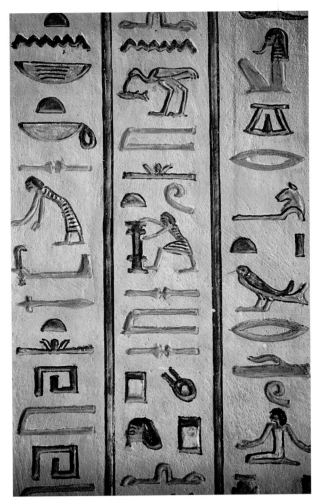

Hieroglyphics on a tomb told
something about the person inside.

Hinduism

see also: India

Hinduism is the oldest world religion. It began in India about 4,000 years ago. Its followers are called Hindus.

Beliefs and teachings

Hindus believe that everyone has duties. The duties are called dharma. Dharma includes things like worshiping God and not hurting other people. Hindus believe it is important to lead a good life.

Hindus believe in a great power called Brahman. They worship Brahman through many gods. Two important gods are Shiva and Vishnu. Each Hindu god has special powers. They have powers over things like money or childbirth. The Hindu beliefs and teachings are written in holy books called the *Vedas*.

This statue of a Hindu god is decorated with flowers.

Hinduism today

There are about 800 million Hindus in the world. Nearly half of them live in India. Hindus worship and pray in their homes and at temples. There are many important Hindu festivals. One festival is Divali. It is the festival of lights. This is when Hindus celebrate stories of the gods overcoming evil.

Festivals are important in Hinduism. The one shown here is honoring the god Shiva.

Hippopotamus

see also: Mammal

A hippopotamus is a very heavy land mammal. Only the elephant is heavier. Hippopotamuses live in central Africa. Hippopotamuses stay in water during the day. They come out of the water to eat grass at night when it is cooler.

HIPPOPOTAMUS FACTS

NUMBER OF KINDS	2
COLOR	brown
LENGTH	up to 11 feet
HEIGHT	5 feet
WEIGHT	up to 7,000 lbs.
STATUS	common
LIFE SPAN	up to 50 years
ENEMIES	Crocodiles sometimes kill baby hippos

a hippopotamus

Hippopotamus families

A baby hippo can swim and walk as soon as it is born. A mother and her young may live together for several years. They live in a group of fifteen to twenty hippos. Each group has one adult male. Other adult males live together in their own groups.

eyes, ears, and nose on top to see, hear, and breathe when in the water

short, wide legs hold up this heavy animal when it is on land

big teeth for fighting; little teeth for munching grass

PLANT EATER

A hippopotamus can walk as much as two miles every night to look for fresh grass.

Hippos wallow in water during the day. The baby hippos are kept safe on top of the adults.

Holiday

see also: Calendar, Festival, Independence Day

A holiday is a day to celebrate or remember something. People celebrate different kinds of holidays in different ways. They may have festivals or parades. People may attend religious ceremonies.

Celebrating culture

Some holidays honor events. Cinco de Mayo is Spanish for Fifth of May. It was the date of a battle in Mexico. Today in the United States, people celebrate Mexican traditions on Cinco de Mayo with feasts and big parades. St. Patrick's Day was originally a religious holiday, but Americans celebrate Irish heritage on that day. African Americans remember their African ancestors with the seven days of Kwanzaa.

Parades are an important part of many holidays.

This is a busy street at Christmas time in New York City.

National holidays

In the United States, there are ten holidays set by law. They are days when government workers get a day off. Other holidays are also special to Americans. Flag Day, June 14, remembers the day the United States adopted its flag in 1777.

U.S. FEDERAL HOLIDAYS

NEW YEAR'S DAY	January 1
MARTIN LUTHER KING, JR.'S BIRTHDAY	Third Monday in January
WASHINGTON'S BIRTHDAY (ALSO PRESIDENTS' DAY)	Third Monday in February
MEMORIAL DAY	Last Monday in May
INDEPENDENCE DAY	July 4
LABOR DAY	First Monday in September
COLUMBUS DAY	Second Monday in October
VETERANS DAY	November 11
THANKSGIVING	Fourth Thursday in November
CHRISTMAS DAY	December 25

Home

see also: Architecture

A home is where someone lives. It is also a place where someone keeps what they own. Many animals also have homes where they sleep and care for their young. About half of the people in the world live in homes in towns and cities. The other half lives in the country.

This house in Ethiopia is built with thatch. This is a traditional way of building houses in parts of Africa.

Types of homes

A person's home can be a house, a tent, a houseboat, or an apartment. Most homes protect people from the weather. A house in a hot country might be painted white. The color white reflects the sun. The color white helps homes stay cool.

Families and homes

Some homes hold a small family. Some homes hold a big family. A family in Africa might have parents, children, aunts, uncles, cousins, and grandparents living together. Their homes are huts inside a walled area. The walled area is called a compound.

Some people live in cities where there is not much space. Lots of homes can be built in a tall apartment building. These apartment buildings are in New York City.

DID YOU KNOW?

People called nomads move their homes from place to place. They live in tents or trailers. Nomads take their homes with them when they move.

Honduras

see also: North America

Honduras is a country in Central America. There are many mountains and river valleys. There is a long coast in the north. There is a short coast in the south. The climate is hot and wet. It is cooler in the mountains.

Living in Honduras

Most of the people live in the mountain valleys and on the coast. Most Hondurans work on farms and plantations. Bananas and coffee are grown to be sold to other countries. Farmers also grow corn. Hondurans eat bananas, coconuts, and shellfish. Tortillas are eaten every day.

These houses on Bay Island are built on stilts. There are wooden walkways between the houses.

The music in Honduras is a mixture of Spanish and local Native American styles. A special style of local dancing and singing is called *garífuna*.

DID YOU KNOW?

Honduras gets its name from the Spanish word that means "depths." This is because the Caribbean Sea off the north coast of Honduras is very deep.

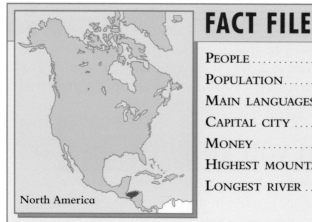

North America

FACT FILE

PEOPLE	Honduras
POPULATION	almost 7 million
MAIN LANGUAGES	Spanish, Native American
CAPITAL CITY	Tegucigalpa
MONEY	Lempira
HIGHEST MOUNTAIN	Mount Celaque—9,273 feet
LONGEST RIVER	Patuca River—199 miles

Horse

see also: Mammal, Transportation

A horse is a large mammal. Some horses can run fast. Other horses pull heavy loads. Horses carried people and goods from place to place before trains and cars were invented. Today many people ride horses for pleasure.

HORSE FACTS

NUMBER OF KINDS	about 100
COLOR	shades of brown, black, gray, white
HEIGHT	up to 6 feet
WEIGHT	up to 2,600 lbs.
STATUS	common
LIFE SPAN	usually 20 to 30 years
ENEMIES	mountain lions, wolves

Horse families

An adult male horse is called a stallion. An adult female horse is called a mare. A female horse usually has one baby at a time. The baby is called a foal. A young female horse is called a filly. A young male horse is called a colt. Some horses live in the wild. They live in groups called herds.

large eyes; one eye can look forward, while the other eye looks to the rear

an Arabian horse

long tail to flick away flies

long, strong legs to run fast or to pull heavy loads

hard hoofs to protect the foot

PLANT EATER

A large horse can eat up to 57 pounds of grass or oats and bran every day.

A mare feeds her foal her milk.

Hovercraft

see also: Transportation

A hovercraft is a type of transportation. It floats on a cushion of air. Hovercraft can move very quickly over land or water.

The first hovercraft

The first hovercraft was built in 1959 by a British engineer. It was a small machine. It carried two people. A large fan pushed air down. The air went under the machine. This made a cushion of air. The machine floated on this cushion. A special skirt was added to keep the air in place under the machine. Later, powerful jet engines were added. Now hovercraft are large and fast.

This is the British engineer, Christopher Cockerell, testing his hovercraft.

How we use hovercraft

Large hovercraft carry people and cars. They are fast because they move above the water. They do not push through water like ships. They also travel quickly over sand and ice, but mostly they travel over water. Hovercraft are used all over the world for short journeys. Hovercraft engines need cleaning often, so they cannot travel long distances. Hovercraft use a lot of expensive fuel.

This large hovercraft carried passengers between England and France.

Human Body

see also: Blood, Heart, Lung

The human body is made up of many parts. All the parts work together.

The human machine

Each of the organs in the human body acts as part of a system. These systems keep the body working. The heart, arteries, and veins are part of the circulatory system. They move the blood around the body. The stomach and intestines are part of the digestive system. They process the food that a person eats. The lungs are part of the respiratory system. They are used for breathing in oxygen and breathing out carbon dioxide.

Healthy systems

All the systems must help each other for a person to be healthy. For example, the muscles in the arm help a person pick up food. Muscles in the jaw help to chew the food. Then the digestive system gets the food. It takes the important things called nutrients out of the food. The nutrients go into the circulatory system. The circulatory system carries the nutrients to the areas in the body where the nutrients are needed.

DID YOU KNOW?

Nearly three-fourths of the human body is made up of water.

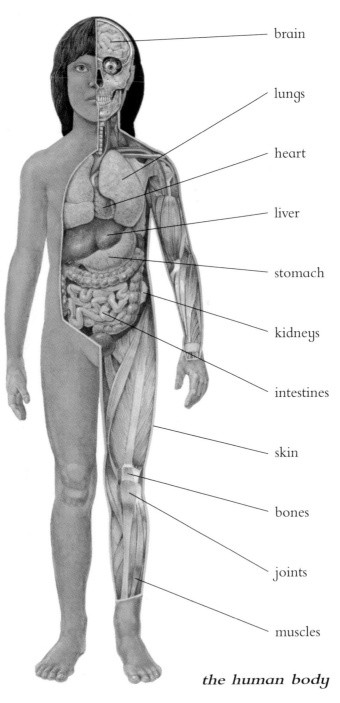

- brain
- lungs
- heart
- liver
- stomach
- kidneys
- intestines
- skin
- bones
- joints
- muscles

the human body

Hummingbird

see also: Bird, Migration

A hummingbird is a small bird. It flaps its wings very fast. It can hover in one place. It can even fly backwards. Hummingbirds are found only in North and South America. Many hummingbirds migrate to warmer places for the winter. The bee hummingbird is the smallest bird in the world.

HUMMINGBIRD FACTS

NUMBER OF KINDS	334
COLOR	mostly bright colors
LENGTH	2 to 6 inches
WEIGHT	much less than an ounce
STATUS	common
LIFE SPAN	about 5 years
ENEMIES	dragonflies, spiders, frogs, people

Hummingbird families

The male hummingbird has a special flying display. He does this to attract the female. The female makes a nest from lichen, bark, and spiders' webs. Then she lays two eggs. When the eggs hatch, she looks after the chicks by herself. She feeds them nectar and insects.

strong muscles to move wings very fast

long beak to sip nectar

colors to blend with flowers

an Anna's hummingbird

PLANT AND INSECT EATER

A hummingbird drinks nectar from flowers. It also eats small insects.

This female ruby-throated hummingbird has covered her nest with mossy-looking lichen.

Hungary

see also: Europe

Hungary is a country in central Europe. Most of the country is lowlands. Many crops grow well in the lowlands. Some mountains are in the northeast. Winters are cold. Summers are hot.

Living in Hungary

More than half of the people live in large towns and cities. The factories make steel, iron, electrical goods, and food products.

Farmers in the rural areas grow grapes, corn, potatoes, and sugar beets. Some people raise sheep and beef cattle. The most famous Hungarian dish is a beef stew called *goulash.* It is made with beef, a spice called paprika, and sour cream.

Tourists visit Hungary. More people visit Hungary each year than the number of people who live there.

Budapest is divided into two parts by the Danube River.

DID YOU KNOW?

The city of Budapest used to be two cities. The cities were on opposite sides of a river. Now bridges link Buda and Pest.

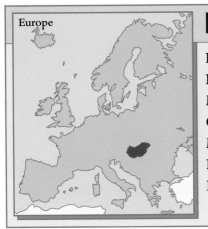

Europe

FACT FILE

PEOPLE	Hungarians
POPULATION	about 10 million
MAIN LANGUAGE	Magyar
CAPITAL CITY	Budapest
MONEY	Forint
HIGHEST MOUNTAIN	Kékes—3,330 feet
LONGEST RIVER	Tisza River—800 miles

Hurricane

see also: Tornado, Weather

A hurricane is a very strong storm. Hurricanes have wind speeds of at least 75 miles per hour. A hurricane can blow down trees. It can damage buildings. It can cause huge waves in the sea. Hurricanes in the Pacific Ocean are called typhoons.

This damage in North Carolina was caused by Hurricane Fran in 1996.

How hurricanes start

Hurricanes begin when warm air rises over a warm ocean or sea. More air moves in under the rising air. The air starts spinning around a center point. This center point is called the eye of the hurricane.

People and hurricanes

People can help themselves be safer during a hurricane. They can use boards to cover glass windows in their homes and shops. They can go to a hurricane shelter. Sometimes people move away from the area until the hurricane is over.

DID YOU KNOW?

Hurricanes are named in alphabetical order. The first hurricane of the year is given a name starting with the letter *A*. The next hurricane is given a name starting with *B*.

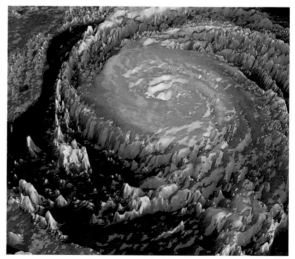

This picture of Hurricane Fran was taken from a satellite. The eye of the hurricane can be clearly seen.

Iceland

see also: Europe, Island

Iceland is an island country. It is northwest of Europe. The Atlantic Ocean is south of Iceland. The Arctic Ocean is to the north. Iceland has many volcanoes and glaciers.

DID YOU KNOW?

There is a warm ocean current called the Gulf Stream. It makes Iceland warmer in the winter than some countries in northern Europe.

Fishing is important to Iceland. The fish are sold to many other countries.

Living in Iceland

Nearly all Icelanders live in towns and cities. Some homes are heated with water from underground hot springs. The hot water is also used to warm greenhouses. Fruit and vegetables are grown in the greenhouses. The hot springs often squirt out high fountains of boiling water. These fountains are called *geysers*.

The most important jobs in Iceland are fishing and making food products from fish. There is not much farming. The soil isn't good enough to grow many crops. Sheep and cattle graze in the countryside.

Music is very important in Iceland. Almost everyone plays an instrument.

Europe

FACT FILE

PEOPLE	Icelanders
POPULATION	294 thousand
MAIN LANGUAGE	Icelandic
CAPITAL CITY	Reykjavík
MONEY	Icelandic króna
HIGHEST MOUNTAIN	Hvannadalsmukár–6,955 feet
LONGEST RIVER	Thjors River–143 miles

Idaho

see also: United States of America

Idaho is a state in the northwestern United States of America. Most of Idaho is in the Rocky Mountains. There are many lakes and canyons in the mountain region of Idaho. In southern Idaho, there is a large plateau. The valleys in Idaho are warm in summer. The mountains are cool and get a lot of snow in winter.

The Snake River winds its way through beautiful Idaho countryside.

DID YOU KNOW?

The largest Native American group in Idaho was the Nez Percé. In 1885, the U.S. government moved the Nez Percé to a reservation. Later, the government took that land away, too.

Life in Idaho

Most people in Idaho live in towns and cities. Some people live in the country and are farmers. They grow potatoes, wheat, and corn. Some people work in mines to extract metals such as silver and lead. Others mine gemstones such as garnets. That is why Idaho is called the Gem State.

Visitors come to Idaho because there are lots of things to do outside. In summer, people camp, hike, and fish. In the fall, they hunt animals. In winter, they come to ski.

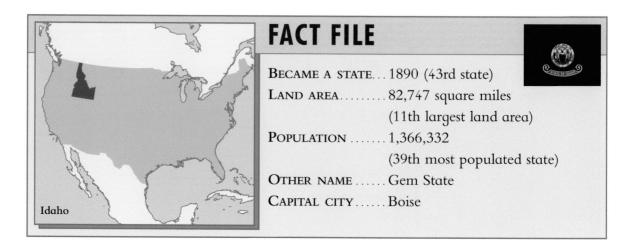

Idaho

FACT FILE

BECAME A STATE	1890 (43rd state)
LAND AREA	82,747 square miles (11th largest land area)
POPULATION	1,366,332 (39th most populated state)
OTHER NAME	Gem State
CAPITAL CITY	Boise

Illinois

see also: Lincoln, Abraham

Illinois is a state in the central United States of America. The land is mostly flat plains and prairie. It is good land for farming. There are hills in the south. Illinois has cold winters and hot summers.

The city of Chicago lies along the shore of Lake Michigan.

In the past

Long ago, thousands of people lived in a settlement at Cahokia, Illinois. The people were the Mississippians. They built large mounds out of dirt. More than one hundred mounds can still be seen at Cahokia.

DID YOU KNOW?

The world's first skyscraper was built in Chicago, Illinois, in 1886. The tallest building in the United States today, the Sears Tower, is also in Chicago.

Life in Illinois

The biggest city in Illinois is Chicago, a busy port on Lake Michigan. Springfield is the capital of Illinois. It was once the home of President Abraham Lincoln. Many people visit Springfield to see Lincoln's home and grave.

There are many factories in Illinois. The factories produce metals and machinery. They also produce chemicals and food. The world's largest cookie and cracker factory is in Illinois. Farmers in Illinois raise pigs, soybeans, and corn.

Illinois

FACT FILE

ILLINOIS

BECAME A STATE... 1818 (21st state)

LAND AREA......... 55,584 square miles
(24th largest land area)

POPULATION 12,653,544
(5th most populated state)

OTHER NAME ...... Prairie State

CAPITAL CITY ...... Springfield

Incas

see also: Aztecs, Maya, South America

The Incas were a native people in South America. They ruled part of what is now Chile, Ecuador, and Peru. They ruled about 500 years ago. The Incas began as a small group in about A.D. 1100. They took over more and more land and people. By 1525, they ruled about 10 million people.

KEY DATES

1100	first Incas settle in the Cuzco Valley
1350	Incas begin to take over more land
1439	city of Cuzco is rebuilt as a capital city
1525	Inca empire splits into two when its ruler dies
1532	Spanish arrive and conquer the Incas

What were the Incas like?

The Incas had a king. He was treated like a god. There were priests, warriors, traders, and other people who were mostly farmers. The Incas believed that many gods and goddesses controlled the world. The Incas prayed to the gods. They gave them presents to keep them happy. Sometimes Incas killed animals and people to give to the gods.

For what are the Incas known?

The Incas are remembered for their beautiful gold jewelry. They are known for their stone roads, cities, and temples. They had a way of keeping numbers on knotted string. The strings were called *quipu*.

What happened to the Incas?

The Inca lands were split between two rulers. Then the Spanish arrived. Their powerful guns and cannons defeated the Incas.

The Inca city of Machu Picchu is now a ruin.

Independence Day

see also: American Revolution, Declaration of Independence, Holiday

Independence Day is a holiday in the United States of America. It celebrates the founding of the nation. It is celebrated on the 4th of July.

The story of independence

Before independence, American colonists were ruled by Britain. They were not allowed to vote for their rulers. They could not make their own laws. In 1775, colonists began to fight British rule. The American Revolution began.

Fireworks light up the sky all over the country on Independence Day.

A crowd celebrates the Fourth of July in Louisiana.

What happened on Independence Day?

Independence Day is not the day Americans agreed to declare independence—that was on July 2, 1776. It is not the day the Declaration of Independence was signed. It is not the day the American Revolution was won. July 4, 1776, is the day American leaders approved the Declaration of Independence.

DID YOU KNOW?

The National Independence Day Parade takes place in Washington, D.C. One of the most popular celebrations is in Boston, where the American Revolution has its roots. The biggest fireworks display is in New York City.

India

see also: Asia

India is a country in south Asia. The highest land is the Himalaya Mountains in the north. The Ganges River flows through a wide valley. There are cool, dry winds for part of the year. There are warm, wet winds for the other part of the year.

Living in India

India has the second most people of any country in the world. Three-fourths of the people live in villages. Most people work on farms. They grow rice. Calcutta and Bombay are big, crowded cities. There are factories in the cities.

The Ganges River is holy to Hindus. People use it to bathe. Ashes of the dead are scattered into it.

DID YOU KNOW?

The world religions of Buddhism, Hinduism, and Sikhism all began in India.

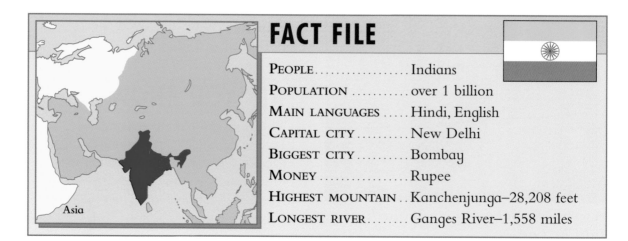

Asia

FACT FILE

PEOPLE	Indians
POPULATION	over 1 billion
MAIN LANGUAGES	Hindi, English
CAPITAL CITY	New Delhi
BIGGEST CITY	Bombay
MONEY	Rupee
HIGHEST MOUNTAIN	Kanchenjunga—28,208 feet
LONGEST RIVER	Ganges River—1,558 miles

Indiana

see also: United States of America

Indiana is a state in the central United States of America. The northern and central parts of the state are mostly flat. In the south, there are hills and valleys. The winters are colder in the north. The summers are warm. Indiana gets plenty of rain.

This is the famous Indianapolis, or "Indy," 500 car race.

In the past

Indiana was named for the Indians, or Native Americans, that lived there. In the 1600s and 1700s, the Potawatomi, Miami, Delaware, and Shawnee peoples lived there. In the 1700s, French people came and built trading posts and forts in Indiana. Some of those places are now towns and cities.

DID YOU KNOW?

The first U.S. long-distance automobile race was held in Indiana in 1911. The Indianapolis 500 is a famous car race today. It takes place every year on Memorial Day.

Life in Indiana

Many people in Indiana work in factories. The factories produce metals and make all kinds of motor vehicles.

Indianapolis, the state capital, is a large city in the middle of Indiana. People in Indianapolis work in offices, stores, and hotels. Some people in Indiana are farmers. Their biggest crops are corn and soybeans.

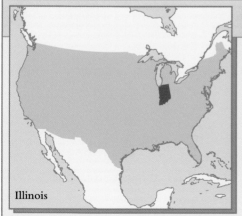

Illinois

FACT FILE

BECAME A STATE... 1816 (19th state)

LAND AREA......... 35,867 square miles
(38th largest land area)

POPULATION 6,195,643
(14th most populated state)

OTHER NAME ...... Hoosier State

CAPITAL CITY ...... Indianapolis

Indonesia

see also: Asia

Indonesia is a country in Asia. It has thousands of islands. There are mountains and active volcanoes on most of the islands. More than half of Indonesia is rain forest. The climate is mostly hot and very wet.

Living in Indonesia

About half of the people work in farming. Farmers cut steps into steep hillsides to make narrow fields. They grow rice. There are many new factories in Indonesia. Shoes, clothes, and other goods are made in the factories. These products are sold all over the world.

There are hundreds of different groups of people in Indonesia. The groups speak different languages. They have different customs.

These village houses in Indonesia are built on stilts to keep cool and dry.

DID YOU KNOW?

The Komodo dragon is the largest lizard in the world. It is only found in Indonesia. It is an endangered species.

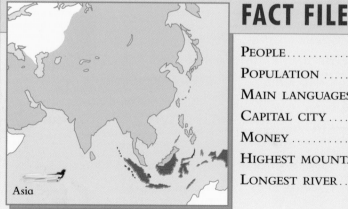

Asia

FACT FILE

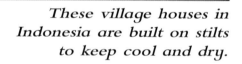

PEOPLE	Indonesians
POPULATION	about 238 million
MAIN LANGUAGES	Bahasa Indonesian
CAPITAL CITY	Jakarta
MONEY	Rupiah
HIGHEST MOUNTAIN	Puncak Jaya—16,505 feet
LONGEST RIVER	Kapuas River—700 miles